BELLS IN OUR LIVES

Tzar Bell In Moscow Kremlin
(opposite) *Bell-founder's Mark: Robert Mot 1570*

BELLS
IN OUR LIVES

Mary Cockett

Drawings by Janet Duchesne

DAVID & CHARLES : NEWTON ABBOT

*Set in 13/14pt Bembo
by Avontype (Bristol) Limited
and printed in Great Britain
by Biddles Limited Guildford
for David & Charles (Holdings) Limited
South Devon House   Newton Abbot   Devon*

CONTENTS

Q.   *Tho' of a great Age,*
I am kept in a Cage,
   Having a long tail and one Ear;
My Mouth it is round,
And when Joys do abound,
   O then I fing [sic] wonderful clear.

A.   *It is a Bell in a Steeple; the Rope*
be-tokens a Tail, and the wheel an Ear.

1

BELLS IN OUR LIVES

How many kinds of bells have you heard today? Does your day start with an alarm clock, a bell mechanical or electric announcing that it is time to get up? There have not always been clocks in private houses.

The telephone bell is part of our ordinary lives in homes and places of work. The telephone is there for use in emergency too. We can summon police, ambulance or fire brigade from a call box in the street. The fire engine still carries a bell, even though its signal may now be a siren. In the past—though customs varied, of course, from place to place—church bells rung backwards were used as fire signals. (Ringing backwards

(above) Antique baby's rattle;
(right) telephone today

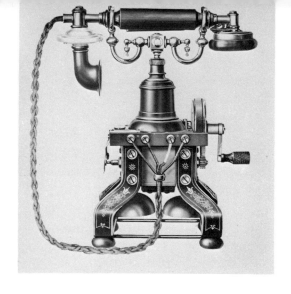

*Magnate telephone,
1910*

means ringing up the scale, ending with the treble instead of starting with it.)

At Woodbridge in Suffolk, according to Eric Rayner in *East Anglian Guide* (June 1970):

> *First you got hold of the clerk of the council, who then found the verger, who then endeavoured to get all eight bells of St. Mary's ringing at once: three cacophonic peals for a fire in the town, two for one in the countryside. This done, and everybody at their doors, the horses were got out from Cross Corner, hitched to the engine and then sent on their errand of mercy, with a great clatter of harvest grinding wheels.*

It is hardly surprising that in old diaries and records everywhere there are many references to buildings being burnt to the ground, especially thatched or partly wooden buildings.

Next time you hear a bicycle bell, remember that in the early days of the bicycle (just before 1900), the 'penny-farthing' was thought so dangerous that a bell hung from the handlebars and rang continuously. After a few years this constant ringing was felt to be unnecessary, and various experiments were made with warning bells for bicycles. Some were so loud they almost startled the lives out of pedestrians. Some rang when a certain speed was reached, others when the brakes were put on.

Some early motor cars had bells, but horns became more popular; their designs were often splendidly elaborate.

Next time you hear a bus conductor ring his bell, remember that there were trams before buses, and the trams (which ran on lines in the streets) had bells—two kinds. The conductor had his bell for giving signals to the driver. The driver had what perhaps could be called a foot bell, in that he pressed his foot on it hard before lurching on his way.

You will hear warning bells at level crossings. Old steam trains carried bells so polished you could 'see your face in them', as a driver said. Engine drivers on local branch lines would ring their bells at certain known places, especially on market days, to warn the walking farmer's wife that she only had a minute or two left if she meant to catch that train and get her basket of eggs to market.

In the days before tractors and trailers, when horses brought in the hay, the hay wain teams of horses wore bells too. They made pleasant sounds down the lanes; but their real purpose was to warn approaching hay teams, for the lanes were too narrow for them to pass. Each set of bells had its own distinc-

Fire engine, London, 1908

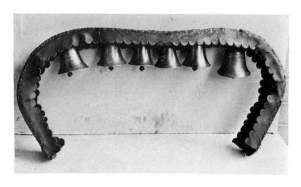

Horse bells. In use up to World War II

tive sound, so that carters could tell which team of horses was coming along and which way it would be turning. It was the waggoners, not the farmers, who owned the bells.

These bells, were hung from an arched wooden frame, sometimes carved, sometimes edged with scalloped leather or fringed braid fixed in position with shiny brass studs. The frame of bells usually rose high over the horses' heads. Keep a look out in museums for the sight of one. There are several, for instance, at the Tunbridge Wells Museum in Kent.

In the days when goods were transported by pack-horses the leading horse wore bells on its bridle—small bells of a shape called crotal.

Now and again, perhaps on a public holiday, you may still see a parade of horses—cart horses perhaps, beautifully groomed, brass shining against the polished leather harness, and again the bells gleaming. But it is a past way of life that is being shown, and there may be more cameras than horses.

I have heard a child say: 'My mother's got an oven bell'. And so she had, but it was what we generally call a 'pinger', a kind of alarm clock which can be set to ring after a certain time—say the time a cake will take to cook. When it rings we are reminded to see if the cake is done.

Nowadays most of us have an oven in our own kitchens. But in medieval England, for centuries during the feudal

Muffin man over fifty years ago

system, the bread oven for the whole village belonged to the lord of the manor. It was in the manor kitchen. When the fire was lit and had reached the right heat, the oven bell was sounded throughout the whole village so that the peasants might know they could bring their loaves for baking. (And the corn they had grown would have been ground—and the grinding paid for—at the corn mill that also belonged to the lord.)

A very familiar bell today is that of the ice-cream man, at places where parents of young children least want him—outside the school gates, for example, at the end of the day. In your grandmother's time it would be the muffin man who rang his handbell, carrying his tray of muffins on his head covered with a clean cloth, generally on Saturday or Sunday afternoons. And not only 'down Drury Lane', as the nursery rhyme says.

Babies still sometimes have rattles with bells on. It is possible to find in antique shops Victorian babies' rattles with engraved

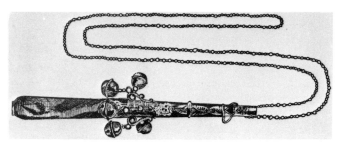

Antique baby's rattle—comforter

silver bells round an ivory ring or a stick of coral that they could cut their teeth on. Museums contain examples of much earlier bell-rattles dating from the seventeenth and eighteenth centuries. And a baby's pram or 'walking-harness' is often trimmed with bells. Fifty years or so ago, in many well-to-do households, a small silver bell stood on the dining table near the lady of the house, so that she could summon the servants to bring in the next course.

Hotels have room bells so that guests can call for service. In old houses you may still come upon a row of bells on springs in what used to be known as 'the servants' quarters'. The bells were wired to the principal rooms, and the servants would know by the number on the wobbling bell where their attention was needed. There are still bell handles or buttons in existence, generally near the fireplace, often elaborately decorated. There were long bell pulls, too, sometimes embroidered. Have you ever pulled the bell at the front door of an old house? How the sound echoes through the place!

Can you think of any animals that wear bells? Donkeys at the seaside almost certainly. Elephants in lumber camps more seriously. Cattle on the mountain sides in Switzerland and Austria and other countries too. In the south of Spain I once stood, one early evening, in remote countryside listening to a host of little bells tinkling. There was nothing to be seen until round the bend of the lane came a flock of fine goats of

Servants' bells in Glasslough Castle

various colours, each one with a bell round its neck. And there, too, was the goatherd and his dog, who had rounded them up from the surrounding hills and was herding them home to be milked. Sometimes, still, the slow, gentle-eyed oxen that draw carts in parts of rural Italy wear bells around their necks. In times when hawking was a sport, hawks wore light silver bells, each with its own sound for easy recognition.

No doubt mice would like cats to wear bells too. A minute's warning would make life more comfortable! The expression 'to bell the cat' has come to mean to do some dangerous deed for the sake of one's fellow men. It dates back to a fable in which a crafty old mouse suggests that a bell should be hung on the cat's neck so that all the mice nearby would hear her coming. A young mouse agrees that it would be an excellent idea, but asks who can be expected to undertake such a dangerous job?

Bells as warnings can sound as pretty as they look. The nursery song, 'Jingle bells, jingle bells', was originally an American traditional song, popular at a time when horse-drawn sleighs were the most effective way of getting about during snow-bound winters. Sleighs, mostly power-driven now,

13

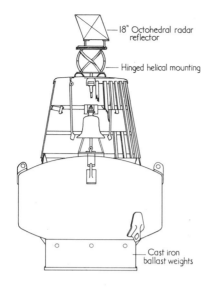

18" Octohedral radar reflector

Hinged helical mounting

Cast iron ballast weights

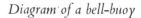

Diagram of a bell-buoy

are still used in some countries with severe winters.

Then there are ship's bells. A ship's bell is fixed, with a rope attached to the clapper, and the clapper is regularly removed and replaced by the bosun or the quartermaster. Otherwise it would ring every time the ship rocked! To a sailor the word 'bells' has a special meaning. The day at sea is divided into seven watches, a twenty-four-hour day starting at midnight. There are 'silent hours' during the night watches, but, apart from those times, the ship's bell is struck every half hour. A sailor's hour on duty, *on watch*, is usually four hours, though there are two watches that only last for two hours each.

Two bells indicate that an hour has passed, three bells that the first hour and a half have gone, eight bells that the fourth hour of watch has been completed.

To quote from the *Manual of Seamanship:*

Except for marking the time the ship's bell is only struck to indicate the position of the ship when at anchor in a fog or bad visibility, or to sound the general alarm in the event of fire or other emergency. The fog signal is the rapid ringing of the bell for about five seconds every minute. For a general alarm the bell is rung rapidly for considerably longer than five seconds, and this is usually followed by a bugle call or a 'pipe' indicating the nature of the emergency and giving orders for dealing with it. The general alarm is only sounded by order of the commanding officer.

At sea, for use in fog, buoys in outlying positions or at important turning points in channels are sometimes fitted with bells, giving warning of reefs or sandbanks. It is a solemn experience, if you are out in a small boat, to come across one of these great buoys, ceaselessly heaving and falling on the swell, incessantly tolling—a melancholy sound.

While thinking of the sea, we may remember the clever seals who are trained to play on bells.

For centuries, and in many countries, people have worn bells when they dance, on wrists and ankles. Morris dancers still dance in English villages, in squares, market-places and on village greens. Have you seen a team of dancers, and heard their ankle-bells?

Probably at school, one of the first 'instruments' you played

Morris men in
Hampshire

in the band was a set of little bells that could be shaken. Bells are used in orchestras, too. 'Tubular Bells', they are called.

Stamp collectors may find they have stamps illustrating bells, for instance an American one inscribed: 'Let freedom ring'.

Before we come on to church bells—making and ringing and all—can you think of other bells in your life? There may be more than you realised. Think what they are for. Think what they mean.

One historic maritime bell is the Lutine Bell, which belongs to Lloyd's of London, who have insured ships all over the world for three centuries. 'La Lutine' was a French warship, captured by the British during the Napoleonic wars and re-equipped as a frigate.

In October, 1799, she was sent to Hamburg carrying gold and silver; most of this valuable cargo was insured at Lloyd's. She was wrecked, with all hands lost, off the coast of Holland. Among the few objects to be salvaged was the ship's bell, which now hangs in the underwriting room at Lloyd's, and is rung to warn members that an important announcement is to be made: one stroke for bad news (usually, in former times, that a ship was lost or overdue), two strokes for good news (that a ship was safe). Nowadays, with improved navigational aids, the bell is seldom heard. It was last rung in February 1972, reporting the loss of an overdue ship.

Bells played by sea-lions (worked by electricity)

2

BELLS AND WORDS

Once you start thinking of bells, you will notice the word where perhaps before you would have thought nothing of it. It appears on inn signs frequently: *The Bell, The Old Bell, Bell Inn, The Bell and Crown, Five Bells, The Eight Bells, Ring o' Bells, Bell and Bottle* and others.

A bell ringer once said to me: 'When you see an old pub called *The Eight Bells*, you can be pretty sure the local church has eight bells'.

As soon as he had spoken, it seemed obvious. Certainly in the past a church with many bells would have been a matter for local pride. The ringing out of those bells over the country-side would attract attention—and trade to the inn. Moreover, ringing is thirsty work: sometimes ringers used to be paid in ale. Also, if they made mistakes they paid a penalty in ale to their fellow ringers. Some churches still have a 'ringers' jug', but usually such jugs have become museum pieces. There was a time when bell ringing fell into disrepute, because the ringers were coming for the beer rather than for the bells.

But to return to inn signs. Bells are a satisfying shape. They

(above) Bell and Crown inn sign

*'Bell-Ringing' by
R Seymour, 1836*

suggest good craftsmanship in bronze, musical sound and a sense of history, and several handsome bells together can make an attractive sign.

You will begin to notice in village and town and on large-scale maps such names as Bell Lane, Bell Field, Bell Meadow. Are they near the church? Bell Field may have been the place where, in medieval days, a hole was dug in which the church bell was cast. Some bells were cast in the churchyard itself. Bell metal and other bell founding remains have been discovered —or uncovered—by grave diggers. Some of them, being bell ringers, understood what they were looking at.

When roads were almost non-existent or very rough, rivers were used for transport whenever possible. If your church was not near a river, it would be cheaper as well as safer to get the bell founder to come to your village than to have the bell cast in his foundry, and possibly cracked on the journey. Some bell founders were itinerant: that is, they moved about the country taking their skill and their tools with them, as tinkers did not so long ago.

If you see Rope Walk near Bell Lane, you could scarcely be luckier in your search for bells and everything to do with them, for where would bells be without ropes?

But you have to be wary of street names and place names. Explanations are not always as simple as they seem. Bell-rope Field at Halstead in Essex is not the field where the rope was made, but it has a connection with bells. The field was a bequest, that is, it was left in a will: the rent from the field was to be used for keeping in repair the bell ropes of the church of St. Andrew.

Similarly, Bell-string Field at Burgh in Lincolnshire was a bequest. It was left in the will of a ship's captain, and the rent from it was to be used for a particular bell—the tenor. And the rope was to be no ordinary bell rope, but of silk. The reason was a good one: it was the tenor that sounded the curfew, and it was the sound of this bell in murky weather which warned the captain that his ship was too close to land for safety.

The word 'founder' needs explanation. It has nothing to do with 'finding'. It comes from the Latin *fundere*, meaning 'to pour, to melt'. It came to mean a man who worked to make or cast objects in moulds from molten (that is, liquified) metal.

Bells are generally well made, and, given decent treatment, made to last. In times of war or religious unrest, orders for new bells are not likely to be given, so the early founders— and indeed, later ones—did not only make bells. The founder was a man who had to be able to turn his hand to other crafts—

Mortar of bell-metal by William Land

the making of mortars, for example. These 'bowls' in which, with a pestle, substances were pounded into powder, were sometimes elaborately decorated. Founders also made keys, crucifixes, pots and pans, ladles and—much later—cannon and cannon balls and guns. Some of the cannon balls fired in the Battle of the Armada, a famous naval battle between England and Spain in the sixteenth century, were made at the Whitechapel Foundry in London, which was also engaged in armament work in World War II.

If 'pots and pans', mentioned above, sound to you a trifle dull compared with bells, remember that they were needed in everyday life, and that some of these 'pots' were beautiful—laver pots, for instance; this is an old expression for a metal jug for holding water. They seem to us more like elegant coffee pots, and were sometimes of complicated design. These laver pots appeared in the trademarks of some early founders, Henry Jordan's, for example. The stylised fish at the top of his shield shows that he was a member of the Fishmongers Company.

In medieval days the word 'yetting' meant 'casting', and many an old bell founder used Belyetere or Bellyetere as his surname. The word and the meaning are still there, though the spelling has changed, in Billiter Street, London. This was the centre of the area in which founding was done.

Here are a few actual names of men who made bells in the distant past:

Bel(l)yetere, John   *Bristol 1236*
Bel(l)yetere, Walter *Bristol 1296*
Bel(l)yetere, John   *Bristol 1300–25*

Trade-mark of William Belyetere
of Canterbury

(right) Parish church, Amesbury, showing louvres

(below) 'A bell is finally a simple shape'. Big Ben, cast at the Whitechapel Foundry 1858

'BIG BEN the great bell of Westminster. Cast at the Whitechapel foundry April 10. 1858.

And there were founders who chose this name at Canterbury, Gloucester, Leicester, Lynn (now King's Lynn), Nottingham, Shrewsbury, Worcester. There was a Robert Belmaker too, possibly of Durham. Other men who worked with metal and made bells called themselves braziers or Brasyer. There were bell founders of this name at Norwich and Bury St. Edmunds.

Note also that potters of the Middle Ages did not work only in clay. They used metal too. York had a bell founder, John Potter (1359–80), and Norwich a Thomas Potter (1404–16).

The word 'bell' comes from an Anglo-Saxon verb *bellan*, meaning 'to bellow'. The Irish for bell is *clog*, the Welsh *cloch*, the French *cloche*, German *glocke*, Scandinavian *klokke*, Italian *campana*, Latin *campana*, and for a little bell *tintinnabulum*. In Pembrokeshire, Wales, there is a hill village Maenclochog

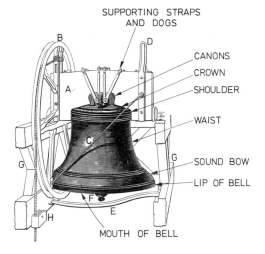

SUPPORTING STRAPS
AND DOGS

CANONS
CROWN
SHOULDER
WAIST
SOUND BOW
LIP OF BELL
MOUTH OF BELL

Diagram of a bell

A - HEADSTOCK
B - WHEEL
C - WHEEL BRACE
D - STAY
E - SLIDER
F - CLAPPER
G - FRAME (partly cut away)
H - PULLEY

(below) Diagram of a bell being moulded

in the Prescelly Mountains. From these hills with their ancient tumuli came the stones for the inner ring of Stonehenge. An early traveller (Fenton) wrote of this village where there were stones that rang like bells.

The word 'belfry', surprisingly, does not find its origin in bells. It comes from an old French word meaning a movable tower that was used for protecting men as they attacked walled cities.

In belfries the openings that broadcast the sound of the bells are called louvres. They are often made of wood, sloping downwards and overlapping, keeping out the worst of the weather, lessening the sound too.

Whenever one begins to look into anyone's work there are

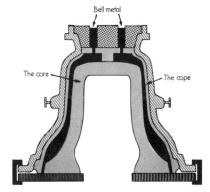

Bell metal

The core

The cope

technical terms that have to be understood. The bell itself is finally a simple shape, but it has a number of basic terms: canons (if the bell is of old design) or 'ears', crown staple bolt, crown, shoulder, crown staple, waist (which used to be lower and much longer in medieval bells), soundbow, lip, clapper, flight. Even the fluffy part of the rope that the ringer holds has its special name—the sally.

The bell hangs bolted to a headstock, once made of wood, now usually of iron. The headstock has metal spindles called gudgeons at its ends, and these, with the aid of ball bearings, allow the bell to swing easily. Long gone are the days when a team of men had to haul at one heavy bell.

Bells are produced by pouring molten metal between two shapes, two moulds clamped together. The inner mould is the core. The outer mould is the cope, even as a cape or *cope* or cloak is an outer garment. Very old bells, both animal bells and church bells, are similar in shape to copes worn by clergy on special occasions. There is a picture of Conrad, Abbot of

King David playing on bells. Early fourteenth century

Canterbury, wearing a cope with 140 little silver bells stitched around the hem, and he is not the only example. And the *Book of Exodus* (xxviii, 33–4) refers to golden bells on the robe of the High Priest.

In the *Book of Zachariah* (xiv, 20), not only are the horses said to wear bells, but there was an inscription on such a bell, 'Holiness to the Lord'. (There are horses with bells on the ancient sculptures of Nineveh too.)

An old German Bible shows King David playing with two hammers on an octave of bells, and looking as though he is enjoying it. Perhaps at school you have played similarly on a row of cups strung up by their handles.

Archbishop wearing cope
(Bayeux Tapestry)

3

IN THE FOUNDRIES (I)

The Whitechapel Bell Foundry, London

It may be that it was in China that the casting process of bells was discovered. They were being cast there five centuries before the birth of Christ.

In the Low Countries (now called Belgium and Holland), bell founding was an advanced craft in the sixteenth and early seventeenth centuries. In those days the making of a big bell was a social occasion, a worrying one too for the founder. Watchers had to be kept back, and prevented from throwing unwanted metal objects into the 'mixture'. There had to be enough liquid metal, and the furnace had to be kept at the right heat throughout. At Antwerp, when the great bell Carolus was founded in the churchyard, the firing took eight days and eight nights. Twenty-eight strong young men took it in turns to keep the heat up, and finally when the bell cooled, it was found to be whole and sound. It was no wonder that feasting followed.

What the bell founder has to do is to make the mould; to melt the metal; to pour the metal into the mould; and then when the metal has cooled and hardened to take away the

(*above*) *The foundry*
(*right*) *Chinese temple bell, 1857*

25

mould, and do any finishing off processes that are necessary. Before the founder can make the mould, he has to make the 'crook' or template or gauge—there are various names—for the shape of the object that is going to be cast.

The crook is made of non-splintery wood that is smoothed and painted. Damp sand in flat trays is then packed firmly round it. When the crook is lifted out, the molten metal is poured in. Different metals shrink different amounts as they cool, so the template-maker (a skilled job, this) has to know exactly how much bigger the template must be than the final object.

But let us get into the foundries. There the processes will become alive in the world in which they belong.

There were once scores of bell founders in England, but bells last well and now there are only two, one in London, one in Loughborough, Leicestershire. Both are very busy making new bells, retuning or recasting old ones, adding to rings (or sets of bells), and rehanging—which often means replacing old-fashioned methods with designs that put less strain on the tower. It ought to be obvious, but it seems not to be, that anyone ordering new bells should have made sure that the

Moulding a modern bell

tower was still strong enough to hold them. It too is likely to be old. It will have endured the strong pull and cross-pull of bells within its confined space, and it may need attention.

The Whitechapel Bell Foundry publishes its own 22 page booklet, rich in photographs and engravings, but it says nothing about its own remarkable atmosphere. Even on a non-working day the visitor can feel it. This is a place of subtle mood and continual pleasant surprise. It is satisfying to know that this foundry has produced bells for more than four hundred years, and other founders' bells rang through

London and far beyond, in the days of Shakespeare, when Elizabeth I was queen.

Enter 34 Whitechapel Road, E.1., and you step beneath the template of Big Ben and templates of two of the smaller bells of the old Bow Bells of London. From the moment of your opening the door—and it opens with a 'ting'—the world of bells takes over. It begins with a display of mainly small old bells, tuned cattle bells, bells for sleigh, hay wain, horse-tram, nursery and monastery. An ancient dragon-ornamented bell from Burma looks lovelier than its sound. Beyond the open door, in what used to be the yard of the *Artichoke Inn*, you pick your way among bells of various sizes. A sundial adorns the wall. Plants thrive in ornamented mortars made of bell metal—another example, you remember, of the founder's craft. A weather vane of a cock, looking surprisingly large at ground level, could not be more right here where the bells, usually on high, are on the ground too. It adds the final touch to this fascinating and unusual picture before one moves into the workaday world beyond the yard.

But even here it is no mere factory. It is far more. One does not take long to realise that this is a way of life. Many factories today are so large, and there are so many processes, that each worker may only do one small, dreary job all day long. What he does is necessary but trivial: it is difficult for him to feel close to what the factory as a whole is producing. In a bell foundry, though each man has his particular job, he knows enough of other people's to understand the whole and his part in it. He is sharing in the creation of something that is worth making, an ancient craft that is still developing.

There is a pleasant, not loud, clanging of metal on metal, made by the blacksmith with hammer and anvil. Before his glowing forge he re-tips a chisel that has been taken red-hot from the fire. A blacksmith in the heart of London!

Across the yard is a large new bell, fixed mouth up on a

28

turntable. It will be tuned by a young man. 'I'm a ringer. The madness caught me early', he says, but he looks as though he has found a way of life where work is something you enjoy doing. The bell has been made as nearly in tune as possible, but now it will be perfected, made harmonically exact. It will be right in itself and it will be in tune with the rest of the ring of bells it belongs to. Listen, next time you hear a bell. Its first sound will be what is known as the 'strike' note, but after it on this and every correctly tuned big bell, comes the hum, which is an octave lower. Listeners with good or well practised ears can detect at least three other notes.

The next bell for tuning is an old one. Lying on its side it shows deep, almost parallel, grooves inside that were chiselled groove by groove. This was the old way of removing metal until the right note was reached. 'The machine will jump when the grooves come round', says the tuner. Often the grooves were roughly made and sometimes chunks of the bell metal broke away. It used to be a perilous business to cast a bell, and a chancy business to tune one. Reputations were lost and made in public. A crowd would gather at a safe distance to watch the founder. It was a great day. Imagine pouring in the metal between the moulds and finding that there was not enough of it, that your calculations had been wrong!

The tuning room

There was no question of sending for more metal and ladling more in. The whole process had to be started again, cope and core unbolted, the part-bell freed, broken, melted down. You can't add to a bell. It must be made in one piece 'at one go'. Imagine tuning a bell in public and letting your chisel dig too deep! A bell might even crack if, for example, the soundbow proved thinner than it had seemed. And a cracked bell is a failure to be dreaded.

Chains rattle, a hook lifts a bell on a trolley and a crane moves it sideways. A cope (the outer casing of the mould) stands in a corner. The cope, dotted with holes that have let out the steam and the bubbles from the molten metal, stands still black from the furnace, its duty done.

The bell itself is not yet the gleaming object you might expect. It has had two days in which to cool, but has not yet been polished. Indeed the solid core is still inside it, the smooth dried loam composed of sand, clay and manure closest to the bell, the coarser loam next, and finally the bricks around which, on a base, the core was built up. Now, with a pneumatic drill, the bricks are being loosened. As the surface of the bell is approached the drill is put down and the work continues with hammer and chisel. Dusty work, this, removing the loam baked to complete dryness. The loam had looked very wet the week before when it was being slapped on to the basic shape, scraped and shaped by a template—more loam, more shaping, little by little until the perfectly sized core was ready.

Out at the back old bells wait, sometimes in whole sets such as those from St. Nicholas Church, Chiswick, greenish, pitted, damaged by weather and time and perhaps by man. This coating of age has already been removed from other bells by shot-blasting or sand-blasting, but nowadays some people prefer them to keep their old appearance on the outside.

There is one ancient bell in for the replacement of its ringing fittings. It came from Whitfield, Kent, and is about seven hundred years old, slim and long-waisted, as bells were in medieval days. Some of its canons have broken away.

There are sparks inside the building as a frame is welded to hold new bells, a new style frame which is light and strong and easy to assemble.

Upstairs in the foundry work goes on continually with a different type of bell—handbells, 2,400 of them, copies of

Modern miniature. A replica of America's Liberty Bell, first cast at Whitechapel in 1752.

America's Liberty Bell destined for the bicentenary of her Independence Day (1976)—one bell for each month of 'freedom'.

The playing of handbells in the States is increasingly popular. A beginning was made when the grandfather of the two directors of the Whitechapel Foundry gave a set of eight bells to a Mrs. Margaret Shurcliff, who went back to America and started a choir.

But it is not to America only that those neat boxes are going, with one carefully wrapped bell in each compartment. They go to Canada, New Zealand, Australia, Israel, Switzerland, and many other countries in sets of from eight to sixty-one, gleaming bells tuned by an electrical tuning unit called a stroboconn. But the tuning and the polishing require human skill. Too high a polish could remove too much metal and change the tone. When clappers and leather handles are fixed, there is, to quote the Whitechapel booklet, 'the final run over. Each set of bells is assembled and tuned as one instrument'. Some handbell ringers wear gloves all the time to protect the bells from becoming tarnished by sticky fingers, and to save the leather from perspiring hands.

There are handbell choirs not only in churches but in schools and youth groups, and the choirs travel about giving concerts, and perform on radio and television. They play classical and popular music as well as church music and carols. Like change ringing, it takes considerable practice, and handbell ringers have their rules too. According to an American writer, the rules include no chattering, no gum chewing, no asking questions without first raising a hand, music to be memorised within seven days, and 'demerits' for unsatisfactory behaviour.

But it is difficult to think ahead to such matters in the busy activity of the place where bells are made.

It seems more important to linger with the work of a nineteenth century bell moulder, W. Thomas Kimber, son of a

'The Great Bell of Bow'

family coachman. Besides being a good moulder, he took it upon himself to copy both the diameter, weight, note, words and decorations on bells that came in to be repaired. These careful drawings were bound into four large volumes, fine in themselves, but useful too. Many bells have been destroyed in war or fire, and in some cases Thomas Kimber's are the only records. Many a church owes it to him that the old inscriptions could be replaced on their new bells.

Among the hundreds of bells replaced by the Whitechapel Foundry were the bells of St. Mary-le-Bow which were destroyed in the Great Fire of London in 1666. You remember the story of Dick Whittington? It was Bow bells, or so the story says, that pealed out: 'Turn again, Whittington!', as he sat despondently on Highgate Hill, prepared to leave London behind him. And he *did* turn back, and found fame and fortune, and became 'thrice Lord Mayor of London'. That was in King Richard II's time.

Some of the inscriptions give the date and the founder only. Some—and how to choose one from so many?—say more: an old bell from North Willingham, Lincolnshire, says in

Latin: 'Grant, I pray thee, that the sound may be as pleasant for me to hear as good for the soul'.

It would feel wrong to leave Whitechapel without giving an example of great personal enthusiasm. Who but one held by the magic of his craft would trouble to follow, as an experiment, the bell founding methods of an eleventh century monk, Theophilus? But this is precisely what was done by Mr. Douglas Hughes, a director of the Whitechapel Foundry, and though the process was long, the eleventh century recipe 'worked'.

It is sometimes possible to visit the foundry, provided you write first to explain the purpose of your visit, and to make an appointment. Their address is: The Whitechapel Bell Foundry Ltd., 34 Whitechapel Road, London E.1.

For further reading I suggest you write for their booklet (current price 15p, plus postage) at the same address. It is called *The Whitechapel Bell Foundry*, and is full of fascinating pictures, as well as clear descriptions of the making, hanging and ringing of bells.

Set of handbells

4

IN THE FOUNDRIES (II)

John Taylor & Co. The Bell Foundry, Loughborough, England

Once there was a cherry orchard where now stand the brick buildings of the largest bell foundry in the world, Taylors of Loughborough. Push open that heavy door, and step into a craftsman's world of which at one time only monks knew the secret.

From here set out on Thursday, May 11, 1882 a bell weighing nearly 17 tons, for St. Paul's Cathedral. It travelled chained to a specially constructed 5 ton trolley, 'and was drawn by a traction engine, another engine following in the rear with the living van . . . Several of the workmen who assisted in casting the bell rode on it through the town'. The route was crowded with people seeing 'their' bell on its way to their capital city. When the procession stopped for the night at Leicester, thousands of visitors, on foot, on horseback, brought by tram or specially hired waggonettes, paid their homage to Great Paul even into the early hours of the morning.

And so the journey went on, not without difficulty from

(above) 'Great Paul' on its way to London's St Paul's Cathedral, 1882. It now hangs in the SW tower

time to time, but never without interest. At St. Albans the Abbey bells pealed out their greeting. There were irritating delays, for in those days bye-laws severely limited the passage of traction engines—in Middlesex 'from eleven at night to three in the afternoon of the next day'. In the metropolis steam traction engines were not allowed to travel after seven in the morning. So, with this and that and stops for Sundays, the bell was twelve days on the road before it reached St. Paul's at eight o'clock in the morning 'just before the roaring traffic of the day had begun'.

The Loughborough workshop is as thick with bells as a market place with stalls. Here have stood new bells ready crated for America, Australia, New Zealand, Nigeria, Jamaica, Barbados, Norway, Jersey and other countries—including, in the past, hundreds to Holland, which no longer imports bells.

It is the old bells that greet one on entry, old bells of every

'Grandisson', the tenor bell of the Exeter Cathedral peal

36

Bell-metal being poured into mould by a ladle

size and many centuries. They stand and wait to be re-cast or re-hung. There are more bells than people, but what to them is a wait of a few months when they have rung away hundreds of years? What have they celebrated, whom have they mourned or called, these weighty sentinels that have watched from on high over village and town? To mention but a few, there were bells from East Pennard, Sidmouth, Long Eaton, Gayton, Nayland ('Henry Plasant Made Me 1698'), a bell of 1407 from Goldsborough, Yorkshire inscribed in Latin: 'Andrew, blessed Andrew, pray for us all', and the ten bells of Chester Cathedral that are to be increased to twelve and will hang in a new bell tower.

Overhead a great girder crane runs the length of the workshop. One man, manipulating the travelling gears (for moving left, right, up shop, down shop, hoisting and lowering), can reach any bell, and calmly hooking it on a chain can raise it—anything up to three tons—and move it where it is wanted.

Many old bells brought to the foundry have to be re-hung because the wooden headstocks have rotted. Some bells have broken canons, but the bells themselves are sound. Some canons, because of the bell's great age or beauty, must not be removed. Or it may be that their owners prefer to keep the original shape, so a new wooden headstock is made, and space for canons and fastenings chiselled out of it, as in the old days. Bells used to be topped with canons or 'ears' because that was the only known way of hanging them. When it became possible to bore holes in bell metal and when the nut and bolt were invented, a good mechanical joint could be made between headstock and bell, and canons were no longer needed.

Everything about the foundry adds to this atmosphere of the world of bells, even the wood-block floors: they are kind to the feet of the workers as well as being a safeguard for the bells. There are clappers long and short and variously coloured hanging on the walls, calipers of all sizes and strange shapes for measuring not merely the size but, at each point, the thickness of the bell. There are crooks, templates, gauges—the terms seem to vary—and there are stacks of bell wheels old and new, wooden wheels of high-grade workmanship.

Here in the woodwork corner are real craftsmen working with obvious satisfaction at creating a new wheel. The 'frame' is of oak, the 'sole' (the channel where the rope moves) is of ash, and elm is being used for the 'shrouding' (the sole's sides, which prevent the rope from sliding out of place). The smell of the wood shavings, particularly wych elm, add to the pleasure. 'And it's a wood you can trust, it doesn't split', says the carpenter.

Across the 'shop' a blacksmith and his assistant, their faces lighted by the glowing forge, work together to 'shut up a clapper'. It is a new clapper, made in two parts, then welded. The scene is worth painting. Here a young man with an oxyacetylene burner, bending over a shower of sparks like a waterfall of fireworks, cuts in seconds a perfect metal circle. It is the beginning of a 'balance weight', which will be fixed to the clapper of a bell in a horseshoe headstock.

Over the road the furnaces deep in the walls are cold at present. A new core for a bell is being built up on a base, loam being slapped on and smoothed and shaped by the crook until the right shape is reached. When the time comes for the bell metal to be melted, the temperature in the furnaces will be raised to about 1100 degrees Centigrade. Then, glowing like a liquid sunset, it will be poured into a ladle—no soup-size ladle this, except in giant terms, for it holds two tons of molten metal, usually composed of about 77% copper, 23% tin. Controlled by hook and chain, by wheel and long handles, the ladle pours its contents into the space between the two moulds, the outer mould, called the 'cope', and the inner core. It is this space that will become the shape of the bell, the bell itself. (See diagram and illustrations on pps. 22, 27, 37.)

Inscriptions require patience and skill. Each letter is tapped with a small hammer onto the inside of the cope, which forms the outside of the bell. Great care is needed not only in spacing but in seeing that the letters—to come out the right way—are placed back to front, and right to left in the correct order for the words. The old founders made many a mistake with lettering.

At the far end of this enormous workshop there is what

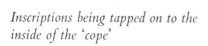

Inscriptions being tapped on to the inside of the 'cope'

39

A 'Carilloneur' at work at his keyboard

seems to be a great room with a raised metal 'door' the width of the room itself; but this is no room, it is the foundry oven where the bell moulds are baked, about 50 ft by 30 ft, and high too. The height is a matter for wonder until you see the base, on which has stood a 15 ton bell for Liverpool's Anglican Cathedral. Its diameter is 9 ft 6 ins. You will have noticed that one does not speak of the height of a bell but of its diameter.

Think of tuning such a bell: it needed the largest of the several tuning lathes, Big Bertha. Gone, long gone are the days when the final tuning was done by chiselling away grooves from the inside of the bell.

Much more could be said about the Loughborough Foundry if space allowed, but we cannot leave it without a particular mention that here are made—woodwork and all—some of the largest and finest carillons in the world. They are used in England, but they are also shipped across the sea in increasing numbers.

While change ringing is not very popular in the USA, the playing of carillons in city halls and churches is greatly enjoyed, and special towers have been built for these instruments.

A carillon [to quote an out-of-print booklet of Taylor's] *is a*

40

set of bells tuned to the notes of the chromatic scale upon which music in two or more parts may be played . . . The bells hang stationary, and are played either by the carilloneur [bell-player] or automatically.

Twenty-five is the smallest number. Unlike the bell ringer, the carilloneur sits as he plays, but it is vigorous work. The keys and the pedals of the clavier are made of wood, the framework (out of sight) of metal, and:

the bells are hung in their framework on different levels, the largest bells hanging in the lowest tier and the smallest in the middle.

Those who like bells but only when they are well played may be pleased to know that there is a 'practice clavier', which allows the player to practise at length without annoying the public.

There must be a special satisfaction in working in one of the few remaining occupations where a man can see from first to last what he is making, and in turning out objects of precision, strength and beauty.

*Carillon chimes in the
cathedral tower of St Rombaut's (Belgium)*

5

WHEN BELLS RING

Nobody is likely even to try to give you a date for when bells began. What is certain is that they have been ringing for thousands of years, on religious occasions and in ordinary life. 'Ringing' does not necessarily mean swinging. Some of the ancient, huge, cylindrical bells could only have been struck with some object—with the clapper if there was one. (And there are other bells such as clock-bells, which are fixed.)

The two main religious purposes of bells have been to announce dying or death and to call worshippers to prayer. As far back as AD 750, Egbert, Archbishop of York, had given orders to priests that bells should be tolled at certain hours.

Monks were called to their prayers at midnight, 3,6,9, noon, 3,6 and 9. Since the various services were announced by different bells, the bells served the purpose of telling the time too. We know from a Saxon cross at Winwick, Lancashire, how an early bell ringer looked and what sort of bells he rang—simple hand bells, one in each hand.

A ringer sculpted in stone on a late Norman pillar at Stoke Dry, Rutland, looks as though his bell ringing is harder work:

(above) This man is playing a strange kind of bell, an iron rod. He is following a priest taking the sacrament to the sick (sixteenth century)

at least he is using both hands.

Ancient civilisations used large bells thousands of years before the birth of Christ and that there were some large bells in England in early centuries we know, for example, from the monk and historian Bede. Hilda, Abbess of Whitby, died in AD 680, and the bell that tolled to announce her death was heard, Bede says, thirteen miles away.

An Abbot by the name of Turketyl gave a large bell, known as Guthlac, to Croyland Abbey in Lincolnshire in about AD 960. But we do not know just what 'large' meant. Who made it is not known, but the monks were skilled in metal working as in many other crafts, and high rank did not exclude such work. For example, the Bishop of Winchester for 963–984 cast bells for Abingdon Abbey.

Bells were given names. The bells of Croyland Abbey had remarkable names: Bartholomew, Betelin, Turketyl, Tatwin, Pega and Bega. Try saying them out loud. Pega and Bega were, as they sound, the smallest of the collection. In 1091 there was a great fire at Croyland. When the abbey was rebuilt, two little bells were given as a present by a copper-smith from Boston (then St. Botolph's town), and his name was Fergus.

Bells are still tolled at funerals, but not now for a dreary length of hours, and usually only a single bell is used. In medieval England funeral bells for one person might

The Bell of St Patrick. Made of iron dipped in bronze (fifth century)

43

boom out every day for thirty days. Not everybody, even in the church, liked it then. There was a Bishop Grandisson of Exeter in the fourteenth century who said: 'They do no good to the departed, are an annoyance to the living, and injurious to the fabric of the bells'. But many people left money in their wills for tapers to be lighted, prayers said, and bells rung for the good of their souls.

When people in high society died the ringing might not only last a long time but take place in several churches. In his invaluable book, *Church Bells of England*, published in 1912 by Henry Frowde, H. B. Walters gives an example from Smyth's *Lives of the Berkeleys:* at Coventry, in 1516, at the funeral of Lady Isabel Berkeley 'there was ryngyng daily with all the bells contynually. There were 33 peals at St. Michael's, 33 at Trinity, 33 at St. John's, at Babyllake 57, and in the Mother Church 30 peals . . . and every pele xiid.'

In the Bayeux Tapestry the scene of the funeral of Edward the Confessor shows two assistant priests, acolytes, following the coffin and carrying handbells. (See illustration at the foot of the next page.) And the custom was not limited to kings. In some places a handbell was rung at the deathbed and the ringer walked through the room and round the outside of the house with the idea of keeping evil spirits at a distance while the soul got safely on its way to heaven.

Before the Reformation bells were tolled not only after

death, but also when a person was dying, so that others, passers-by as well as close friends, might pray for the departing soul. If you heard a bell tolling in twos it was for a woman, if in threes for a man.

Someone had to be paid for tolling, and there is evidence in the Churchwarden's Accounts of many churches. In 1526 at St. Mary Woolchurch in London:

Item the clerke to have for tollynge of the passing
bell for manne womanne or childe, if it be in
the day   *os. 4d.*
Item if it be in the night, for the same   *os. 8d.*

But more was paid for long ringing or for heavy bells, or sometimes for other special reasons. For example, in 1572 at the Church of St. John the Baptist at Peterborough the then large sum of eight shillings was paid 'to a poore old man and rysing oft in the nyghte to tolle . . . the wether beyng grevous'.

Imagine the gloom of the death bell during times of calamity such as the Great Plague, when thousands died. Here is an entry from Samuel Pepys's *Diary* for July 30, 1665: he is writing about the church he attended, St. Olave's in Hart

Funeral of Edward
The Confessor,
showing men with
handbells

Street, London.

It was a sad noise to hear our bell to tell and ring so often today either for death or burials; I think five or six times.

Except in poor parishes many churches had several bells, but often each bell was used for one purpose only. The Sanctus bell, for instance, in medieval days, was rung three times as the choir sang in Latin: *Sanctus, Sanctus, Sanctus, Dominus Deus Sabaoth.* 'Sanctus', you will remember, means 'Holy', and the bell was sometimes inscribed with three Ss. The rope usually hung near the altar so that it could be reached easily. The bell was usually outside, so that it could be heard also by those who were unable to come to church. They then knew what point the service had reached and could join in silently.

The Sacring bell was rung at the Elevation of the Host. Sometimes, more often on the Continent than in England, it was a single bell. Or, as at Gerona in Spain, there might be several bells fixed to a wheel that was pulled by a rope. One of the largest was at the Abbey Church of Fulda in Germany, an early sixteenth-century brass wheel, twenty-four feet across, star-shaped, with fourteen points, and carrying about a hundred and fifty little bells.

A Sermon bell indicated either that the sermon would shortly begin or, in Elizabethan times, that there was a qualified preacher in church that day. Puritans sometimes came in only in time for the sermon, and they liked their sermons long in those days—two hours or more.

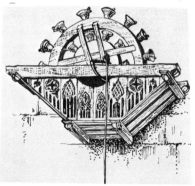

The Ave bell, rung at four or five in the morning, was to call you from your bed and to your prayers before a working

Wheel of the Sacring Bells at Gerona

46

day that began very early.

The Curfew bell, sometimes a Town Hall bell, sometimes a church bell, is still used in times of trouble such as civil war or oppression to warn people off the streets. It was used in the eighth century in England, in King Alfred's time, to remind citizens that it was time to cover their fires with a sheet of metal for safety and to end the day and go to bed.

The curfew bell has had many uses. It signalled closing time at ale houses. More importantly, it gave warning of the closing of town gates in days when towns were encircled by walls. Those who did not belong to the town were reminded by the bell that they must have someone to sponsor them or they might be called on to explain what they were doing in the town after the gates were closed.

In past times bells were rung on occasions of importance in the countryside. There was the bell to mark the cutting of the first sheaf of corn, the bell that rang as the last load of the harvest was brought home, and the gleaning bell; and bells are still rung in many places for the harvest festival service. Customs must change when most people live and work in towns. Pancake Tuesday (Shrove Tuesday) used to be a general holiday, and the bells rang then far and wide. After that day, that is during Lent, the bells rang only for services until Easter Day.

They are still rung on New Year's Eve, muffled before midnight. At that hour, if there is no church clock to speak for itself, the tenor, unmuffled, rings twelve strokes, and then, all mufflers off now, the treble leads the rest of the bells to spread the sound of joy and to welcome in the New Year. (Mufflers, usually made of leather, are put over the clapper to soften the blow on the bell.)

Bells whose work has been confined to everyday matters, such as announcing the beginning of a church service, come into their own if there is some important occasion, a Coronation, a Sovereign's birthday, the arrival of an important visitor, the end of a war. In World War II church bells were silenced.

When communities were smaller, bells in some villages were rung for the birthdays of leading families, such as the lord of the manor. Bells still ring out at weddings, too, of course, if they are asked for and paid for, providing there is still a practised band of ringers to honour the occasion.

For centuries bells were used to announce the opening and closing of markets. In medieval York the Corn Market was held in a wide space called Pavement (with wheat on the north side, rye on the south side, etc.) and part of an order by the Mayor and Corporation made in 1550 reads: 'Nor to sell in the market place before the Corn Bell . . . be rung at 10 o'clock'. It was illegal to sell in advance, it was illegal to sell outside the market place. Honest traders were thus protected; besides, the city would have stood to lose part of its revenue if selling outside had got out of hand. Now a trader pays rent for his stall or his pitch, but then a toll was charged for the selling of goods in the city, for example, two dishfuls, that is, two pints, from every sack of corn. Some markets still open with the ringing of a bell.

There are bells of the past whose absence we have no reason to regret. But many people want to photograph or buy postcards of the place where the Town Crier stood to announce the news of the day. Are they trying to recapture the sound of his bell and the kind of news he gave out? Think of the way we receive our news today, how far it has come, what kind of news it is, and compare it with the town crier's of old. You may possibly come across some of the news announced by your local town crier in the past—not from a modern ceremony in fancy dress, but from some document, something he actually said. Town criers are still occasionally employed in some country towns, mainly for their historic interest, and as a tourist attraction.

In all these uses of bells, and there could be more, we have

(left) Wells Cathedral. 'Jack Blandiver', a large quarter-jack; (right) Wells Cathedral. Two knights above a clock strike the quarters

not even touched on the old, widespread beliefs in their magic properties. Bells can still act as warnings—of storm, fog, invasion—but few of us now believe the bells to have magical powers of their own. Nevertheless, for centuries people had faith that bells could ward off harm. Perhaps this is because bells were associated with the church from early times, and were dedicated, made holy, in special ceremonies.

It used to be thought that storms were brought about by evil spirits, by fiends in the air. Bells, it was thought, could frighten these 'creatures':

the bells ben rongen when it thondreth and when grete tempeste and outrages of wether happen, to the end that feinds and wycked spirytes should be abashed and flee, and cease of the movynge of the tempest.

This quotation is from *The Golden Legend*, by an early printer, Wynken de Worde.

Malmesbury Abbey had a special Storm Bell. If you had no special bell, your ringers made as much noise as they could with what they had, and certainly the more din the bells made the less the thunder would be heard, and presumably you shut your eyes against the lightning, as many people do now. The ringers were paid for such ringing. There are many accounts to prove it.

Some bells did not limit their powers to dealing with the weather, if one is to take notice of their inscriptions. Many a bell carries some such wording as this: *Voce mea viva depello cuncta nociva.* (With my living voice I get rid of harmful things.) It is a brave claim. And note that word 'living' voice. Bells *spoke*—well, many people believed that they spoke.

Some bells carried an inscription against the deadly dreaded Plague. *Pestem fugo* (I put to flight the plague), claims the fifth bell at Guilsborough, Northamptonshire, and it was not only English bells that made such declarations. Probably they were meant as prayers, but perhaps it was felt that a firm statement is stronger than a plea. Also a bell was a symbol. It was believed by many that it spoke with the voice of the holy priest and that God spoke through him.

Space must be spared for bells that chime the hours, and for those strange figures known as quarter-jacks, quarter-boys or Jack-of-the-clock that strike the quarter bells.

At Rye, in south-east England, in the turret of the Parish Church of St. Mary the Virgin, is a clock that was made in 1560. The quarter-boys were added two hundred years later—two fat gilded wooden cherubs, each with a pivoted arm raised ready to strike. And strike they did until 1969, when they were replaced by fibre-glass copies. The originals, repainted, stand inside by the Clere Chapel windows.

The Old St. Paul's Cathedral that was destroyed in the Fire of London had clock jacks at least as far back as 1298.

Inside Wells Cathedral, Somerset, visitors gather to watch

the fourteenth century clock which shows the date of the lunar month, twenty-four hours, the minutes and the state of the moon. Every fifteen minutes in summer (on the half-hour in winter) four jousting knights on horseback ride on their private roundabout; one, suitably hinged at the waist, is knocked backwards on his horse. A black metal disc in the centre of the clock is meant to be the earth with crinkled edges to represent clouds. To the right of the clock, high on the wall, sits a large quarter-jack known as Jack Blandiver. With his heels he strikes bells that hang under the seat.

Outside the Cathedral, above still another clock, two knights in fifteenth century armour strike the quarters on two bells with their halberds.

If you look carefully you may find the small figure of a fifteenth century bishop's jester. He has no bells, because he is in mourning for the bishop. His face and his whole posture suggest great sadness.

Wells, to quote from *The Friends of Wells Cathedral:*
has the heaviest ring of ten bells in the world. The weight of a ring is determined by the weight of its tenor bell. The Wells tenor, known as Harewell, of 56¼ cwt. is the 5th heaviest ringing bell: the heaviest tenors—at Liverpool, Exeter, St. Paul's and York—all belong to rings of twelve. (Certain chiming bells such as Great Paul at St. Paul's, Big Ben, Great George in Bristol University tower, and Great Tom at Oxford are very much heavier, but, of course, they do not revolve.)

Many places have elaborate and beautiful or strange clocks, with jacks or their equivalent—Strassburg, Orvieto, Munich, Leipzig, and in New York the building of the New York Herald. It is difficult to select a few out of so many.

Before the days of household clocks people seemed to feel affection for these quarter-jacks who measured out their day, and even now grown-ups as well as children wait patiently for the mechanical figures to perform upon their bells.

6

WHERE BELLS HANG

In many countries, particularly in the past, bells hung in towers separate from the church—bell towers, called in Italy *campanili*. There are two at Ravenna belonging to the churches of St. Apollinare in Classe and St. Apollinare Nuovo. They are round towers with pairs of arched openings near the top, and they date from between the seventh and the tenth century.

A campanile known throughout the world is the one in Venice in St. Mark's Square and just across from the Doge's palace. It has been part of the life of the city since 912, Venetians say, when its building was begun, suitably, on St. Mark's Day, April 25. Cannon have been fired from it. Welcomes have been sounded on its bells. The deaths of criminals have been tolled on the crime bell, called *Maleficio*. Councillors in the past got to their feet and trotted on mule-back to their meetings when the bell called *Trottoria* sounded its call. A lift will now take you to the top of the campanile, but Galileo walked up when he went there to demonstrate his great invention of the telescope.

The campanile, 324 ft high, was built, like so much else in Venice, on piles, for Venice is a city built on islands. But it

(above) Bells of St Paul's Cathedral, London

52

seemed firm and sound until July 1902. Many a Venetian will tell you of the 'tragedy' as though he saw it himself only a week or so ago, he makes it so vivid. The fall was not absolutely sudden. For a few days in advance those in the know gave warning. The usual midday cannon was not fired because of danger from vibration. Even the bands outside the famous cafés in the square (the Piazza) were not allowed to play. At dawn on July 14, 1902 the Piazza was closed, and the caretaker of the campanile and his wife took up their possessions and departed to a safe distance. At five minutes to ten that morning the campanile, which had given a view over Venice and the lagoon to millions of people, shook a little, gave not much more than a shudder, and almost in silence crumbled to the ground. When the mountain-high cloud of dust had settled, one large bell, the *Maragona*, was found unbroken.

That evening the Council met, and it was decided that the campanile must be rebuilt *com'era*, *dov'era*, that is, as it was, where it was. And there it is today, lighter in weight but

(left) Ravenna. Campanile, Church of St Apollinare in Classe. (date between seventh and tenth century); (right) Venice. Campanile in St Mark's Square

Bell-house at East Bergholt, Suffolk

looking almost as it did, and Pope Pius X himself paid for the melting down and re-casting of the broken bells.

This true story was told me by an old Venetian lady in Venice itself.

Many countries still have their separate bell towers, leaning perhaps, but still standing. Ireland has a fair number of round ones and Great Britain too, but the only old English cathedral still to have a campanile is Chichester. Saxon bell towers were built in England as early as the seventh century, at Hexham, for example. In Saxon England, as in other countries in their early days, the best and probably the only stone building in the village was the church, so it had to serve too as a place of safety from raiders. Some churches had round or, as at Ramsholt in Suffolk, oval towers built close against the church, but without a staircase. They had two or more floors, but access was by ladders inside, and you would hope to pull up the bottom one after you in case of pursuit.

Many great churches—look at their ground plans—are built in the shape of a cross. A tower may rise in splendour from the centre, but sometimes when the tower is supported by a system of arches instead of by solid walls, its weight has proved too much. This is what happened at Winchester in 1107, at Ely also and at Bury St. Edmunds. Central towers in many countries have collapsed.

A superb example of a central bell tower is that of Tewkesbury Abbey.

It would be wrong to give the impression that a church could not have bells unless it had a bell tower. The bell's chief function is to make an announcement, and that can be done, less splendidly, admittedly, without a special building towering on high. What simpler than to do as is done sometimes in poor countries still—hang a bell from the bough of a tree? This was customary in England in bygone years. Or if for some reason a tower could not be built, a frame in the churchyard would hold the bells. Indeed the church at East Bergholt in Suffolk (village of the painter John Constable), houses its bells in the churchyard in a 'cage' under a low roof. But such a position gives no joy to those who like their bells to ring out 'to the wild sky', or to those who like to feel that the bells are poised between earth and heaven.

Different types of English bell towers: (above left) oval tower of Ramsholt church in Suffolk; (below left) a bell-cote, Partrishow church, Brecknock; (right) a flint tower at Burham Thorpe, Norfolk

Many churches have a western tower—the early eleventh century church at Earl's Barton, Northants, has one. Some churches have two towers, some three, some a spire, some both tower and spire, some a dome, like St. Paul's Cathedral, in London. Some, especially on the Continent, have a wealth of towers and spires on a single church. Occasionally a stone turret rises over the east end of the nave.

There are small churches which have no tower or inner way of approaching the bells, but merely a little bell cote; they can be severe-looking, but are often pretty and ornamental. There are plenty of these pretty bell-cotes—sometimes called 'birdcage towers'—in Scotland, mainly dating from the seventeenth century.

Many churches have an open turret at the gable end, often with two bells. It may even be over the eastern end of the nave, as at West Littleton in Gloucestershire.

Most towers are made of stone, brick, or flint and brick; but here and there is a tower of wood infilled with some other material, and there are bell turrets made all of wood, like that of the thirteenth century church at East Wellow, where Florence Nightingale is buried. There are Mission churches in Africa with towers made of thin, straight tree-trunks interwoven with reeds; they used the only material there was and took a lot of trouble in the process.

Perhaps one of the oddest places for a bell to hang is in the open mouth of a totem, as it does at Wharkarewarewa, Rotorua, in New Zealand.

An example of a central bell tower, Tewkesbury Abbey, Glos.

7
SEARCHING OUT THE BELLS

The ringing chamber—that is, where the ringers stand—
is usually up in the tower just below the bell chamber.
Or it can be on the ground floor, perhaps behind curtains,
or unscreened, as at Hewelsfield in Gloucestershire, where the
ringers are in full view.

The lower ends of the ropes are looped back or tied. Often
there is a notice: 'The bells are up. Do not touch the ropes'.
Whether or not there is a notice, behave as if there is, but take
a look round the ringing chamber. It may offer much or
almost nothing of interest. Perhaps you will find framed
notices of names of men who have rung for forty or fifty
years, and even longer. There may be proud records of the
lengths of peals the ringing team or band had achieved in this
or other churches.

In the ringing chamber in a church in Maresfield, Sussex
there is a rhyme, dating back to about 1770, a set of Rules
for Bell Ringers in verse neither better nor worse than many
found in ringing chambers:

(above) Washington Cathedral Bells
(Washington DC)

If that to ring you do come here
You must ring well with hand and ear
If that you ring with spur or hat
A quart of ale must pay for that,
And if a Bell you overthrow
Sixpence is due before you go,
And if you curse or swear I say
A shilling's due, without delay.
And if you quarrill in this place
You shall not ring in any case.

In Somerset and other cider making counties, the quart would have been of cider.

I have never seen a notice saying what the neighbours thought about bell ringing that went on ceaselessly for hours. I have been told once or twice, but the words might burn the paper. Perhaps it is safer to put it in the words of a parish clerk in a place where bell practice used to start at six o'clock on Sunday mornings:

I wish for the peace and quiet of these lands
That ye had round your necks what ye pull with your hands.

And this parish clerk was not alone. In the eighteenth century there was a church bell in Hammersmith, London, that used to ring at five o'clock in the morning, and so dis-

turbed the sleep of residents that two of them (Dr. Martin and Lady Arabella Howard) made a bargain with the church

Carving on bell tower of New College, Oxford.

*Old print showing
ringing chamber and
bells hung in tower
(No separate
bell chamber)
'The way to the bells
may be by ricketty
ladders'*

authorities. If the early bell ceased to ring, they would present
the church with a new cupola and a new clock. That bell
stopped ringing in the year 1724!

There may be in the ringing chamber written details and
photographs of the hanging and dedication of new bells.
The ceremony will vary from church to church, but ceremony
it certainly is—blessing of water by a Bishop, the sprinkling
of this water on the bell, sometimes the anointing of the bell
with oil, and hymn-singing meanwhile.

You may discover the weights and sizes (diameters) of the
bells, and the name of the founder or founders. If his name is
not there, his trade mark or stamp may be given, and a list of
founders and their marks can be sought out. But a mark cannot
always be relied on, for sometimes on the death of a founder

his stamps and tools passed to someone else.

Not all ringing chambers produce interesting information, but when they do you will have found it the easy way. Searching out the bells themselves, even if you have permission to do it, can be cold, dirty and dangerous work. When you get to the bell chamber itself, the floor may well be slippery and spattered with the droppings of bats and birds—owls, pigeons, jackdaws and so on—and messy with their feathers. The bells too will probably be encrusted and corroded, and you may not after all be able to read a word or see a design.

It would have been better to say: 'If you get to the bell chamber', for the way up is sometimes very difficult. There may be a staircase, but the steps may be worn or broken, and a good torch is likely to be needed. But there may not be a staircase. The way to the bells may be by ricketty ladders with missing or broken rungs. Trap doors between the floors may have stuck. Unless someone has been up there not long before, the release of the trap door could bring down a shower of dirt and a stone or two.

The towers may be narrow, so that the ladder has to be almost, even quite, vertical. Occasionally there is not even a ladder, but a succession of stumps—or are they staples?—sticking out from inside the wall, and even they may not start from ground level.

Many bell-cotes are without any inside approach. Anyone who had to attend to those bells would have to reach them by outside ladders or scaffolding.

Now and again, as a means of raising money, some churches open their towers to the public. There may then be a chance for you to see the bell chamber, but *never* try to go up without permission, or alone. Bells, for a number of reasons, can be dangerous—or if not the bells themselves, some weakness in the roof or the hanging.

There is a warning in a booklet of the Central Council of

Guildford Cathedral bells ringing

Church Bell Ringers that reads:

> *When you see a bell in action you will realise why you must (1) NEVER go alone among bells that are 'up' (mouth upwards) and (2) NEVER touch a bell rope if there could possibly be anyone among the bells.*

You may find in your Reference Library a book or local history notes on bells. They may also have Parish records.

And, with a bit of luck, you may here and there find an old bell in a place where you can easily have a good look at it, such as the ancient bell, now replaced by Taylor of Loughborough, which stands in the churchyard of Tickencote church, Rutland. There is one on the floor of St. David's Cathedral, Pembrokeshire, at the western end and not in a good light—cracked, and with a chip out of it, but old and large. At St. Mary's, Tenby, in Pembrokeshire, beside the marble tombs of Tenby merchants in St. Thomas's chapel, stands a bell with fine canons ('ears') and the name Sancta Anna. The date is about 1500, and the founder's initials (round a crown) are R T, of Bristol. The Sancta Anna used to hang outside the spire, and for many years was used as a curfew bell.

Some bells announce plainly what their purpose is:

I ring at six to let men know
When to and from their work to go.

But often old bells bear a saint's name, usually the saint to whom the church is dedicated. The Church of St. Peter and St. Paul, Chaldon, Surrey, used to have two bells, called 'Peter' and 'Paul'. You may also find the mark of the founder (if you are lucky), and perhaps a Latin inscription. Between each word may be some decoration, perhaps a flower, or a square cross, sometimes plain, sometimes richly ornamented. Latin inscriptions frequently include the word for 'holy': *sanctus*, *sancta* or *sancte*. (If you don't learn Latin at school, get someone who does to explain the difference.) Like many other words on inscriptions, it is often shortened, so the early ones are not easy to read.

There are some interesting modern inscriptions on bells given by the United States to Eriswell in Suffolk, where there is an American Air Force base:

Americans Gave Me
John Taylor Made Me   April 17, 1958
God Protect Those Who Fly
May Anglo-American Friendship Never Die   April 17, 1958
May this bell forth tell
Glory to God in Eriswell   1958

If you see on a bell an angel, a lion, a bull or an eagle, do not look among the founders' marks for them. They represent, in that order, Matthew, Mark, Luke, and John.

IHC and IHS stand for Jesus. They are shortened forms of the Greek for Jesus.

Those who are more interested in design than in words will enjoy the richness of some of the early Gothic lettering or other decorations—royal heads, for example, at least, heads with

*Founder's mark. Taylor of
Loughborough*

crowns on. The right to use them is said to have been granted
to certain founders by Kings or Queens reigning at the time;
Edward III and Queen Philippa are two. But as I have said
earlier, founders' marks changed hands as the years passed.

Not all inscriptions are of great interest in themselves.
You will be lucky if you find one as delightful as that on the
treble bell at All Saints' Church, Nottingham:

> *I mean to make it understood*
> *That though I'm little yet I'm good.*

But there may be some other aspect, such as the proud
dignity of the words on Gloucester Cathedral's seventh bell:

> *I have the name of Gabriel,*
> *who was sent down from heaven.*

Perhaps you will think of it next time you see pictures of the
Annunciation. (And Gloucester has the only large medieval
bell left in England: Great Peter dates from the fifteenth
century, and took eight men to ring it in the days when it
was raised. It was 'great' when it was made, but many bells
both of church and city weigh more than twice as much as
Great Peter, at 2 tons 18 cwt.)

If you start collecting inscriptions, you may find some that
commemorate a historical occasion. A hand-written account of
the Bromsgrove Foundry states that in the famous octave or

63

set of eight bells in St. Helen's Worcester, 'none of the bells required any chipping or filing'—a tribute to the seventeenth century founder, Richard Sanders. The inscriptions on those bells were in memory of the battles and achievements of the Duke of Marlborough. Another Worcestershire bell, also made by Sanders, is inscribed: 'Thomas George of Overbury gave this guinny'. The gold coin, a guinea, had been impressed and cast on the bell.

At Northfield, Warwickshire, bells 1 and 2 make it clear that there had been some argument before the new peal was made:

     1. We now are six tho' once but five.

     2. And against our casting some did strive.

It is interesting that though the bells were ordered for church use, and blessed and dedicated with some ceremony, the inscriptions were sometimes far from holy. The founders often took the opportunity of inscribing in bronze how good they were at their work and how poor some other founder. Even the great Rudhalls of Gloucester were not above it, that family who from 1684 to 1830—Abraham, Abraham II, Abel, Thomas, Charles, John—made well over four thousand bells before they were bought up by the Whitechapel Foundry in the nineteenth century. Abel inscribed on a Gloucestershire bell at Badgworth:

     Badgworth ringers they were mad

     Because Rigbie made me bad

     But Abel Rudhall you may see

     Hath made me better than Rigbie. 1742.

But it is more than likely that the inscriptions you find will spell out something similar to some part of this old rhyme:

     To call the folk to church in time

          We chime;

     When mirth and joy are on the wing

          We ring;

At the departure of a soul
We toll.

A more cheerful inscription, and one that turns up time after time, is: 'I sound not for the souls of the dead but for the ears of the living'. It is usually in Latin: *Non sono animabus mortuorum sed auribus viventium.*

At Buxted Parish Church, Sussex, approached along an avenue of old trees, there used to be six bells. There are eight now. But in the summer of 1971 there were no bell-ringers to use them.

The inscription on Bell No. 7 is simply:

William Hull made mee 1686.
11 cwt. G

'G' means that the bell is tuned to that note in the scale. The 15 cwt tenor (F) is inscribed:

At proper times my voice I'll raise
And sound to my subscribers praise.

The names of the subscribers who paid for it are not stated. It might have been a long hard struggle to collect the money in the parish; often a cart was pushed round to receive unwanted metal objects suitable for being melted down to add to the bell-metal. It was in Buxted, in 1543, that an ironmaster, Ralph Hogge, cast the first English cannon in one piece. Whether he made bells too is not clear.

At Bath Abbey a bell says precisely whom we ought to praise:

All you of Bathe that heare me sound
Thank Lady Hopton's Hundred Pound.

Bell border used by Abraham Rudhall

8

THE ART OF
CHANGE-RINGING

Church bells can be rung in several different ways. The
simplest way is called 'chiming', in which the bell remains
hanging downwards. Then there are 'ringing in rounds'
and 'change-ringing'. If you look at the diagram of a bell
and its fittings on p. 70 you will see that they are designed
so that the bell can be turned right over, and also stopped in
the upward position, as is necessary for rounds and 'change-
ringing'. Ringing in rounds is comparatively simple: it means
that the bells are rung in the same order again and again,
beginning with the treble bell, ending with the tenor bell.

Change-ringing is very much more complicated. I could not
attempt to explain in detail how it is done; and indeed a
handbook for beginners in the art of change-ringing stresses
that it can only be learnt in the ringing chamber itself, when
you have seen the bells and had their working explained.
Bell-ringers are enthusiasts in the practice of their difficult
art, and are happy to undergo feats of endurance during a
prolonged peal. What was it, do you think that kept the
Ancient Society of College Youths on their feet in the belfry of

(above) Guildford Cathedral bells 'raised' and ready to ring

66

St. Matthew's Church, Bethnal Green, London, for nine hours and twelve minutes, ringing out 15,840 changes? And a peal at Earlsheaton, Yorkshire, lasted thirty-eight minutes longer.

'It's the sport of it', said one young ringer recently, 'and being in a team. If it catches you young, it's got you for life'. 'They have a power over you, bells', said an old man, his hands raised towards the rope. 'That Everest, now, I'd never want to bother with it. It's bells for me'.

Not all churches have teams of bell-ringers. But perhaps you are fortunate enough to live near one that does, and can listen when the bells are rung. Listen carefully and you will begin to hear a pattern in the sound, where at first all you heard was a wild clangour. Try to keep listening to the same bell all the time, picking its sound out from the rest—the number of bells varies from church to church. The bell you are concentrating on will seem to be chasing the others, and sometimes will be overtaken by them, weaving their musical patterns. No wonder these patterns are called 'changes', with every bell changing its place, every bell 'hunting' others.

Or so it seems to us, standing outside. Inside, in the ringing chamber, every member of the ringing team knows exactly what he has to do. Just as the car driver should with practice develop road senses, so the bell-ringer learns 'ropesight'. It means being fully aware of the ropes, knowing whose turn comes next, taking your correct place in the pattern, in the 'change' that is being rung. For in change-ringing the bells do not follow the same order, but follow a predetermined arrangement.

As a very simple example, look at this one, which is called the 'Plain Hunt'. Try to imagine keeping your place exactly at the right time if you were Bell Number 1.

2 1 3

2 3 1

3 2 1

$$\begin{array}{ccc} 3 & 1 & 2 \\ 1 & 3 & 2 \\ 1 & 2 & 3 \end{array}$$

Now, on a piece of paper, try tracing the path of each bell.

Suppose there were six or eight bells or more. If you like mathematics, you will probably enjoy the complications. (If you don't, I suggest you skip this part!) Remember that the same bell cannot be rung immediately again: it turns over and has to be given time to get back to its starting position. In change-ringing a bell may keep its place but generally it moves one place each time. So the ringer does not need to know every word of the poem, as it were, but he does need to know who comes before him.

The following is a change for five bells. Read the columns downwards, that is, 12345 then 21345. The bells ring one after another. Notice that each bell moves one step at a time, and that by the end the bells are in the order in which they began.

12345	32451	43512	54123	15234
21345	34251	45312	51423	12534
23145	34521	45132	51243	12354
23415	34512	45123	51234	12345
23451				

This is a Stedman method, and a very simple one compared with some of his. Any bell-ringer will know the name of Fabian Stedman, born about 1631. He was a printer's apprentice who became very interested in bell ringing. In the mid-seventeenth century it was popular and fashionable to join

Ringers in a ringing-chamber

68

a Ringing Society. The one Stedman chose was the Schollars (so spelt) of Cheapside, in London. He became tremendously involved in ringing and in working out mathematically complicated 'changes' of bells. In 1668, helped considerably by a rector, Richard Duckworth, he brought out a book, *Tintinnalogia or the Art of Ringing* (Kingsmead Reprints, Bath, 1970). Change-ringing flourished. By the eighteenth century it was almost a form of sport in England, and one in which men on all levels of society could join.

The various changes or 'methods' had their own titles—bob minor, Kent treble bob major, grandsire double, grandsire triple, names which would set off excited conversation among ringers. There were competitions too, sounding very like endurance tests of physical toughness as well as of skill in ringing changes.

Enthusiasm grew, bells were re-cast, bells were added—sometimes to mark a special occasion, sometimes, it would seem, because one little town could not bear to be beaten by another. Painswick, a beautiful town in the Cotswolds in Gloucestershire, had had a Society of Ringers since 1686. By the eighteenth century the church had ten bells, but when a neighbouring town increased its peal to ten bells in 1815 after the Waterloo victory, Painswick saw to it that before very long its own church had *twelve* bells.

Pride and jealousy about the number and weight and splendour of bells have been felt in places large and small and in many countries.

The three photographs of bells at the end of this chapter will give you some idea of the complexity of change-ringing, and the skill and accuracy necessary to control each movement of the bell. Fig. One shows the bell hanging down. Before beginning to ring, the ringer will raise the bell to the 'up' position (Fig. Two)—and very carefully this has to be done. Fig. Three shows the bell 'up' but at 'backstroke', slightly tipped back, i.e., when the ringer momentarily releases the rope, before pulling on it again. (If you look back to the picture of bell-ringers in the ringing-chamber, on p. 68, you will notice that each ringer is holding the 'sally', the fluffy part of the rope, or the rope itself, either higher or lower than his fellow ringers, each knowing that his bell, high above his head and unseen in the bell chamber, is in one of the different positions which the bell travels through over and over again during the ringing. The bell, in change-ringing, begins and ends in the 'up' position. But at every stroke the bell travels round—makes a complete revolution.

If you would like to know more, you might write for *An Elementary Handbook For Beginners In The Art of Change-Ringing*, published for the Central Council of Church Bell Ringers, the address is: Mr. and Mrs. Drew, Monsal, Bredon, Tewkesbury, Gloucestershire.

Bells in three positions during change-ringing

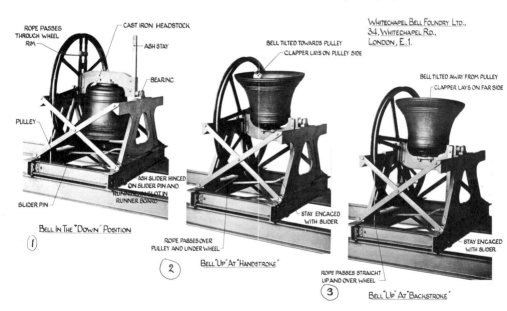

9

YOUR TURN NOW

You may be fortunate enough to live near a great abbey which keeps a long record of its bells. York Minster, for instance, has bell records that go back as far as 1371 when, it is recorded, £60. 10s. 10d. was paid for work on the bells— a large amount of money six hundred years ago. In the north aisle of the nave the minster has a triple window that was given by a founder Richard Tunnoc in the fourteenth century, and each window is bordered with bells. Two windows show methods of making small medieval bells. The other shows Richard Tunnoc himself, a mayor of York and a Member of Parliament as well as a founder. There may be some of his bells still in existence, but if so it is not known which they are.

Or you may be a Londoner; in which case you will have no lack of opportunities for your search. Why not take the nursery rhyme, 'Oranges and Lemons' and see if you can find out where the churches are that come into the song, or what has become of them? St. Clement Danes, in the Strand, still rings the tune on its bells, restored by the Whitechapel Foundry. If you are old enough, or can persuade an elder brother or sister to come with you, you could spend a whole holiday travelling round, using the useful 'Red Rover' bus tickets.

(above) The first Big Ben arrives at Westminster

Dunwich, E. Suffolk. Once a thriving English town, gradually swallowed up by the sea

These are but two examples of countless places where a great deal of pleasure is to be had searching for bells and everything to do with them. There are even bells under the sea. If you live in Suffolk you may know the story of Dunwich, once a thriving town which was gradually swallowed up by the sea—churches, houses and other buildings. All that remains are a few cottages and the ruins of a Franciscan priory. Legend has it that fishermen, on a still night, have heard the church bells tolling, rocked by currents. Do you live in some other place where the church has been covered by water? There are places where valleys, villages and churches have been drowned to make reservoirs to provide water for the towns. Mardale Church, which used to stand at the head of Haweswater in Westmorland, was allowed to fall into ruins for ten years before being finally engulfed. When the level of the lake is low you can still see the top of the tower.

But even if you do not live near a church old enough to

have a long history, somewhere in your area, in church records, perhaps kept in the church, or in any library with a local history collection, there is likely to be something about bells—their cost, argument as to whether to have them at all, their date, their founder and his name or mark, details of their hanging and dedication, and, if you are in luck, their inscriptions.

In medieval times founders in many countries dated their bells—in the Low Countries (Holland and Belgium), for instance. But in England you will be lucky to find one dated before about 1570. In the ringing-chamber, you may come across copies of the inscriptions on one or more bells. Do not be too surprised if you find the odd letter back to front, or upside down, or out of place. Many old founders were good craftsmen, but not necessarily at home with the written word. Besides, as I described in Chapter Four, think how skilled they had to be in impressing the letters on the mould of the bell.

At Castle Combe in Wiltshire one bell in the Church of

Mardale church, at the head of Haweswater in Westmorland, dismantled before the valley was flooded

St. Andrew has an inscription commonly used, *Ora pro nobis* (Pray for us), preceded by an invocation to Saint Peter (Sancte Petri). But the founder went wrong on 'sancte'. The 'a' and the 't' are upside down and the 'c' has been mistakenly placed after the 's'.

The second bell also bears a common inscription:

I to the church the living call
And to the grave do summon all. A.R. 1766

The initials stand for the famous founder, Abraham Rudhall of Gloucester, who was also an enthusiastic bell-ringer. Sometimes he placed a small bell sign between the A and the R on his stamp.

Bell stamp of the famous founder,
Abraham Rudhall of Gloucester

The hunt for inscriptions, or anything to do with bells, can lead to some strange discoveries. You may come upon foreign bells, taken as spoils of war, or ships' bells from wrecks that have found their way to church towers or schools. One bell that has 'come home' is that of Brunel's *SS Great Britain*. It was handed back by the Falkland Islands after being used for a hundred years to call sheep to the fold. The reunion took place when the old ship had been towed to Bristol.

Many old bells, some from parish churches, mostly from monasteries and nunneries, were taken down when Henry VIII ordered the Dissolution of the Monasteries. Some bells disappeared. Most were smashed to pieces and melted down for sale as gun metal, much of which was sold overseas, though a law was passed (often broken) against exporting it. But some bells were taken down and hidden, under a floor, say, or bricked up in the corner of a wall. Bells have been found in ponds, thrown there, perhaps for safety, until better times.

You may find a bell that by its ringing led some lost person to safety. But there were also bells that rang in fog or darkness, not to guide, but to lure lost travellers in order to rob them— and they might be lucky to get away with their lives. I know of a farmhouse that was once equipped with such a bell of evil purpose.

You yourself may come across a bell that seems to have been donated for a reason that seems strange to us today. For example, in the year 1544 the seventh bell at St. Peter's, Nottingham, was given by Margery Doubleday. Many rich people have given bells, but Margery Doubleday was a washer-woman. She left 20s. a year to the sexton, for which he was to ring the bell every morning at 4 o'clock to awake the other local washerwomen. Her bell was meant as a kindness and a service to her friends in the days when there were no clocks in ordinary houses. Where had she done her washing? Down on the banks of the River Trent chatting as people now do in launderettes? What was she like, this Margery Doubleday? Doesn't it leave you wondering? Is there an account of her somewhere? Has she descendants who know about her? Or is she remembered simply by that seventh bell?

In the same century as Margery was doing her washing by day, the City of London employed watchmen by night. They sounded their bells at regular intervals, called news of the weather, and gave their blessing, sometimes in verse, as they passed by. They are not all nameless. One, Isaac Ragg of Holborn, London is shown in a woodcut in the Luttrell Collection of Broadsides at the British Museum. He carries a pointed pole in one hand and a bell in the other, and a lantern (very necessary before the days of street lights) is fixed on his jacket.

Annals of Bristol, prepared in the eighteenth century by

John Latimer (re-issued in 1970 by George's of Park Street, Bristol), records the purchase of a new watchman's bell:

In the civic accounts for 1707 is a payment to John Packer, founder, who charged 14s. for 'a bell for ye bellman, for ye yous of the sitty, made of newe mettell', and 8s. for 'new casting and turning the bellman's bell.'

But 'a ould bell waying 6 lb' was traded in, and for this Mr. Packer allowed 4s. 6d.

What you are looking for in your local bells depends on your kind of interest: it may be musical, engineering, artistic, a study of beliefs or attitudes in different centuries. It may be architectural—the architecture of the tower in particular. It will be a rare find if you come upon all such information in one book, as I was fortunate enough to do in a Bristol publication by St. Stephen's Press (1928), *History of the Ancient Society of St. Stephen's Ringers, Bristol* by H. E. Roslyn.

The first St. Stephen's Church was built in the thirteenth century on swampy ground beside the River Frome, outside the Norman walls that enclosed the city. The district was at the mercy of quarrelling barons and of pirates who sailed up the Avon. The church was mainly rebuilt in the fifteenth century, but the early church, too, had bells. Some of the contributions towards them were in the form of goods rather than money, in wine, for example, and in woad. The woad would be used in the dyeing of cloth. You can't read for long about Bristol without coming upon cloth and ships: one of the Bristol bell founders had a ship on his trade mark. Edmund Blanket, who was among the first to get looms working after cloth weaving started up again seriously about 1331, had a link with St. Stephen's. In 1371 he was granted a royal licence to found a chantry chapel there. Whether blankets have their name because he was the first person to make them is not certain.

St. Stephen's has one of the most stately and beautiful

towers in England. Delicate battlements and pinnacles rise above its four stages. It was the splendid gift of Master John Shipward, twice Mayor and once Member of Parliament for Bristol in the middle of the fifteenth century.

Exactly when bell ringing began there is not clear, but the church had its band of ringers before Queen Elizabeth I visited the city in 1574.

There were five bells, then eight, now ten. Number eight announces: 'We were all cast at Gloucester by Abell Rudhall 1759'. The other two were added by Llewellins and James of Bristol. For those who want diameters and weights, all are given in H. E. Roslyn's book.

Inscriptions on the older bells are:

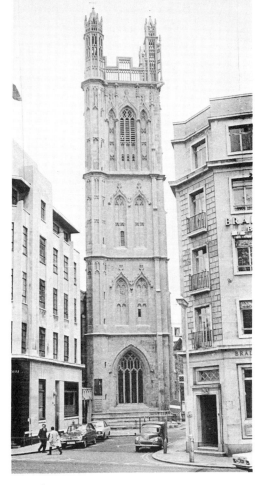

> *God preserve our Church and State.*
> *Peace and Good Neighbourhood.*
> *Success to the British Armies.*
> *May the Trade of the City Increase.*
> *Prosperity to this Parish.*

Never, even on the bells, is one allowed to forget the importance of trade.

Well, the bells rang with zest, and in 1905 the gracious tower was showing signs of wear. Architects found a slightly bulging wall, loose stones, cracks in the oak beams that carried the floor of the bell chamber . . . and 'the part of the frame that carried the two heaviest bells was not quite upright'.

Clearly something had to be done. It was suggested that Taylors of Loughborough should be asked to put in steel girders and frames, but a bell ringer managed to persuade the committee against metal. As wood was also cheaper, the ringer won his argument.

The Society of St. Stephen's Ringers was precise in its rules, and there were many. Here are only a few: a member shall pay a penalty if he:

miss to strike his bell at the second sway;

speak or make any manner of noise when the Bells do ring;

take a rope out of a fellow's hand when the bells do ring well and do make a fault;

quarrell or misuse any of the said Company.

If any of the said Company shall be so rude as to run into the Belfrey before he do kneel down and pray as every Christian ought to do, he shall pay for the first offence sixpence and for the second he shall be cast out of the Company.

So that was a fair warning! Like every kind of teamwork

ringing carries its own discipline and its own rewards.

There is teamwork among the ringers and teamwork among the founders, but often—you cannot fail to notice if you start looking—the architect seems to have given very little thought either to the men who had to make, hang, and maintain the bells or to the men and women who ring them. Of course the tower or the spire must be a thing of beauty, but inside it is for use too. (Not, I must add, that this criticism applies to St. Stephen's.) If you become an architect, the bell founders will both thank you and regard you more highly if you keep them and their needs in your mind and on your plans.

Whatever country you are in, old or new, bells there must be—or whatever is used instead of bells—silver trumpets maybe, or a sea conch, wooden rattles, tree trunks hollowed out. You may see small china bells that tinkle in the breeze in houses, or bells of glass—yes, even of glass, part plain, part coloured, and often patterned too. And if you hear a barrel organ or a disc musical box, there could be a bell there also.

A small book can only start you off on a subject with so long a history, but Good Hunting!

SS Great Britain

ACKNOWLEDGEMENTS

Author's Acknowledgement
to two English bell founders

To Mr. Douglas Hughes of Whitechapel, London and Mr. Paul Taylor of Loughborough.

I offer particular thanks for the way in which they gave of their time and knowledge, and then allowed me the freedom to go where I liked and ask what I liked in their workshops. Thanks are certainly due too to the men who worked there and who so patiently answered my questions.

The publishers would also like to thank Mr. Paul Tayor for technical advice, and Miss Diana Lodge for her painstaking research in finding illustrations.

Also Mr. L. S. Colchester, Secretary of Wells Cathedral. The Reverend M. W. Dittmer, Rural Dean of Chippenham, Wilts. Trinity House Corporation, London. Lloyd's of London.

Thanks are due to the following for illustrations.

Novosti Press Agency — frontispiece; the Post Office — pp 7 and 8; Radio Times Hulton Picture Library — pp 9, 23, 18, 42, 43, 52, 59, 68, 71; University of Reading Museum of English Rural Life — p 10; the Mansell Collection — pp 11, 24, 45; Trinity House — p 14; J. Allan Cash Ltd — pp 15, 21 (top), 53 (rt), 55 (left and rt), 56; Whitechapel Bell Foundry — pp 16, 21 (lower), 22, 25, 26, 27, 29, 30, 31, 33, 34, 37, 39, 57, 61, 66 (photos on pp 27, 29, 37, 39 by Terry Rand); ERD Publishing Ltd — p 17; Belgian National Tourist Office — pp 40, 41; Jonathan Robertson — p 49; John Taylor & Co — pp 35, 36, 63; Horniman Museum — p 25 (lower); Foto Enit, Rome — p 53; Barnaby's Picture Library — p 55 (upper left), 72, 73; New College, Oxford — p 58; Bristol United Press — p 77; Bristol City Art Gallery — p 78.